Gainsborough Old Hall

A guide to Gainsborough Old Hall
by Sue Allan

Almost hidden away in the north-west corner of Lincolnshire,
magnificent Gainsborough Old Hall is one of the most impressive
and best-preserved medieval manor houses in England.

Built by the noble Burghs, the Old Hall has been owned,
as well as lived in, by just one other family,
the Hickmans who arrived in Gainsborough in 1596.

With muted reds of warm Tudor brickwork set against
romantic black and white timber framing, this grand old lady of Gainsborough
has stood watch over the town and River Trent for more than five centuries.

Architectural features

For the greater part, the construction of
Gainsborough Old Hall is of
timber-framing as can most readily
be seen within the interior (and
exterior) of the Great Hall, one of the
oldest parts of this building.

The English oak for this was almost
certainly sourced locally from the great
swathe of forest that once formed a part of the
surrounding Old Hall estate. Trees with a natural
curve in their growth would have been especially
sought after in order to construct the great arched roof beams.
Samples taken from these in the Great Hall suggest that these
oaks were felled somewhere around 1460. The fact that ugly cross
braces were not used to support the impressive timber arches,
has endowed the Great Hall with a serene and almost church-like
feeling.

The spaces between the timber uprights used to build the walls
were in-filled horizontally with pieces of wood called 'laths'.
In turn these were then covered over with 'plaster' consisting of
a mixture of such things as dust, horse hair, lime, lime-ash and
animal dung in several coats of decreasing coarseness. At the time
this was a very common form of building construction:

Hickman-Bacon family crest

*"The greatest part of our building in the cities and good towns of
England consisteth only of timber, for as yet few of the houses of the
communalty (except here and there in the west country towns) are
made of stone….'these english"*, quoth he (a Spaniard of Queen Mary's
day), *"have their houses made of sticks and dirt, but they fare
commonly so well as the king."*

William Harrison, Description of England, 1587

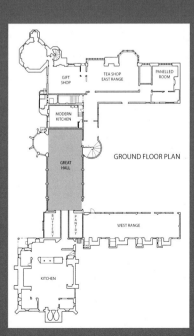

The floor of the Great Hall would have originally comprised of compressed earth which was probably then consolidated by the addition of a layer of fresh ox blood. The floor tiles in situ today are a later addition.

Looking towards the end of the hall there are three doorways: the centre one leads to the kitchen flanked by the buttery and pantry to the right and left. Originally these functionary rooms would have been partially shielded from the view of the Lord's table by a huge screen that once spanned the far end of the hall. There might also have once been a minstrel gallery above. Although the screen has long since been removed, marks can still be seen in the timbers where it was once attached. Below is an impression of how the screen might once have looked.

Heating for the Great Hall was by means of a central fire. Set into the roof above there was once a 'louvre' to draw smoke and fumes upwards and out of the building. (The framework of the original louvre turret is now upstairs next to the tower bedroom). The louvre also let in additional light. The Lord and his table would have enjoyed extra heating by means of portable braziers.

The bay window of dressed stone or 'ashlar' does not appear to have been especially designed for the Great Hall. It is of late perpendicular-style with fine two light tracery of such high quality that suspicion arises that it must have been looted from a dissolved religious house after Henry VIII's break with Rome. Because the vault is clearly late Elizabethan or Jacobean, it has been suggested that it was therefore inserted at that time.

Stained glass panel

However, equally plausible is that the structure was originally incorporated into the hall much earlier during the 1500's but then needed repair later. In any case, the inclusion of this window was intended as a sign of wealth and to cast extra light upon the high status end of the hall.

In early photographs two stained-glass panels can be seen still in place in the bay window. During the 1960's, one bearing the royal coat of arms, was removed and framed, albeit inside out.

Originally the other windows, set high on each side of the Great Hall, would not have been glazed. Glass was a highly expensive commodity in the C15th and when used, if the Lord of the Manor travelled away from Gainsborough for any length of time, it would have been removed and taken with him. Instead of glass, linen coated with a mixture of sheep fat and wax could be used instead for windows. In bad weather this could be supplemented with wooden window shutters or hides to keep back the wind and the rain, however with the consequent loss of much natural light.

...e Function of a Great Hall

...e notion of a great hall, a large principal room in ...istocratic domestic buildings has existed from pre-Saxon ...mes and on into the Tudor/Jacobean era. Over time this ...eveloped from being an independent building into instead, ...at Gainsborough Old Hall, the heart of a large house. ...would have served also as the hub of the estate with ...eople constantly coming and going. At Gainsborough Old ...all, the Great Hall with its kitchen would have been built ...st.

...early times, ordinary folk attached to the wider ...ousehold depended entirely upon the Lord of the Manor ...r their every day existence, often working for their 'keep' ...ther than for pay. As a result, it was usual for household ...embers to come inside their particular great hall at the ...d of the day. On locking the hall doors for the night – the ...remony of 'All-night' – the household would then settle ...own to sleep communally. For medieval people, darkness ...d the night were a fearful time when trouble, robbers, or ...nger lurked, or when even ghosts or evil spirits might be ...road! It was this idea of there being safety in numbers ...at bore overriding consideration, far above any idea of ...ersonal privacy'. In fact at this time the concept of a ...droom as we know it today was unknown.

...nid this communality, there would have been a strict ...cial pecking order understood by all, as to where one ...uld and could not go within the Great Hall itself. There ...uld have been a 'lower end' to the hall (with services ...ached such as the kitchen) and the socially lower order ...the household would remain in that part.

...en there was an 'upper end' to the hall, the focal point of ...ich would have been the Lord's high table set upon a ...is and beneath a large canopy. This area was only for ...ose 'closest' to the Lord and it was at this end were the ...rd's accommodations were (such as the private ...thdrawing area known as 'The Parlour'). Set beside the ...is would be the Lord's 'buffet' – a sort of cupboard – on ...ich the family plate of either silver or gold would have ...en displayed as a sign of his great wealth, again not a ...ace for the lowly to be found straying.

Great Hall roof and colourful heraldic banners

The floors of the Great Hall would have been strewn with rushes – or 'thresh', which soaked up spillages and made the environment more comfortable. It was also very practical as it was easy for soiled thresh to be gathered up and replaced with new.

Beds for the lower orders of the household consisted of a sack or 'tick' woven from hemp that would then be filled with hay (hence the saying 'hitting the hay' for going to bed). Moreover, ordinary medieval people often slept with their heads on a log for support.

The great central fire (along with others in the rest of the house) had to, by law, be put out at night at around eight o'clock. The Law 'couvre feu' was designed to help protect buildings from accidently burning down at night as people slept. This led to our modern word 'curfew'. However, once the flames were out a large earthenware cover (also called a couvre feu) could be placed over the hot embers thus safely keeping the heat going for long after.

The other main function of a great hall was as a place for the household to take its main meals.

However, once the West Range at Thomas Burgh II's newly completed manor house was built, Gainsborough Old Hall would have run upon much more sophisticated lines. At 'All-night' only sworn members of the Lord of the Manor's staff, family or special guests would have been allowed to remain inside the Manor House, and mostly these occupied the West Range.

By the late 1400's, in keeping with the practice of other noble families, Lord Burgh and his family would have by far preferred to have kept themselves as distant from their common servants as possible and undoubtedly remained within their luxurious private apartments much of the time.

The Great Hall is where banquets would have been held. Imagine the Great Hall; a riot of colour with brightly decorated flags hung from the roof and with everyone dressed in their finest clothes. Minstrels would have no doubt made merry music as course after course of the finest foods were introduced to the diners accompanied by the fanfare of a trumpet.

Status would dictate each person's place at these meals. Therefore the higher your status then the nearer to the Lord's table you were seated. The nearer to the Lord that you sat, the higher was the quality of the meal you received. Even what your meal was eaten from depended upon your social standing and therefore might range from a slice of stale bread to a wooden trencher or onwards up to plates made of pewter, silver or even gold.

Table etiquette of the late 15th and 16th centuries was also surprisingly strict and fellow diners would scorn any breach made. Although knives and spoons were used for most courses, for taking food from communal dishes fingers sufficed, hence an important part of good manners was to be seen washing one's hands before helping oneself to such food. Thus dishes of water scented with herbs or flower petals water accompanied by towels were proffered to diners at intervals throughout the meal.

Visitors of Note

On October 10th, 1483, King Richard III stayed the night at Gainsborough Old Hall on his way to London from York. However, shortly after this his host, Thomas Burgh II, appears to have switched his allegiance to the King's Lancastrian opponent, Henry Tudor, and soon Richard would be dead.

In August 1541, King Henry VIII visited Gainsborough Old Hall on his way from Lincoln to York. 'Letters and Papers, Foreign and Domestic, Henry VIII 1541' show that the King left Lincoln on the Friday (12th) for Gainsborough and meetings of the Privy Council are recorded as having taken place at Gainsborough on the 14th, 15th and 16th – showing that Henry stayed at the Old Hall for three days.

It is not clear if Henry and Queen Catherine Howard actually slept at the Old Hall during those nights or not. At Lincoln it is recorded that: 'The King and Queen came riding into their tent, which was pitched at the furthest end of the liberty of Lincoln, and there shifted their apparel, from green and crimson velvet respectively, to cloth of gold and silver…' However, after a service at the Cathedral it was then also noted 'Then all went straight to their lodgings for the night…' suggesting that the royal party probably did not sleep in their tents but indoors elsewhere.

If Henry and Catherine slept within the Old Hall, then several chambers might well have been deemed suitably fine enough to accommodate them. However, contrary to popular belief the king is unlikely to have used the upper bedchamber in the tower. By this time Henry was very obese and his long-standing problem of painful, ulcerated legs would have made it extremely difficult to climb the narrow staircase.

eat Hall bay window

ater history of the Great Hall

y the end of the Tudor era, the Old Hall no longer paid
ost to royal visitors. By William Hickman's time, the Great
all had become little more than a yawning, little-used
pace with his lordship quietly dining elsewhere.

et this was by no means to mark the end of the Great Hall's
sefulness. John Smyth's Gainsborough congregation of
eparatists may have gathered in this place for their meetings
hile it is known that John Wesley certainly once preached here.

ven after the Hickman family had abandoned the Old Hall
s its family residence in the 1700's in favour of a new hall at
honock, the Great Hall continued to be used as a public
enue, a fact that no doubt led to its ultimate survival into
odern times.

t first, the Great Hall served as the town's public hall. Then
1790 Mr. West, an entrepreneur, leased the Great Hall and
ted it out as a theatre, complete with seats and a gallery.

hen the then owner Lady Frances Hickman died her
uccessor, Henry Bacon Hickman, wanted to refurbish the
reat Hall and turn it into the Corn Exchange. However the
eatre continued on for many years until in 1849 it was
eported; 'the theatre... has been demolished, the large
anqueting hall in which the theatre was fitted up, is to be
estored'.

y this time the Old Hall in general was in a very poor state
nd so railway engineer, Denzil Ibbetson, was engaged to
ndertake repairs. Ibbetson was responsible for the cast iron
orbels that can still be seen today at the lower ends of the
ched roof braces in the Great Hall. It was also about this
me that the Great Hall's north door was replaced with a
indow and the woodcarvings made.

Burgh Family Time Line

Thomas Burgh I
Died 1432

Thomas Burgh II
1432-1496
Built Gainsborough Old Hall

Edward Burgh
c1464 –1528

Thomas Burgh III
C 1488-1550
Chamberlain to Queen Ann Boleyn

William Burgh
1522-1584

Thomas Burgh IV
c1558-1597
Sold Gainsborough Old Hall

Hickman Family Time Line

Lady Rose Hickman
1526-1613

William Hickman
1549-1625
Bought the Old Hall 1596

Willoughby Hickman
1604-1649

William Hickman
1628-1682

Willoughby Hickman
1659-1720

Neville Hickman
1701-1733
Built new hall at Thonock

Neville George Hickman
1725-1781

Lady Frances Hickman
1747-1826
On death the Old Hall passed into Bacon family

Henry Bacon Hickman
1788-1862

Sir Henry Hickman Bacon
1820-1872

Sir Hickman Beckett Bacon
1855-1945

Sir Edmund Castell Bacon
1903-1982

Sir Nicholas Hickman Ponsonby Bacon
b1953-
President of the Friends of the Old Hall Association

Buttery & Pantry

These two service rooms are situated either side of the central passage leading towards the kitchen.

Pantry comes from the French word for bread, 'pain' which indeed would be amongst other items of cold, cooked food temporarily stored in this area prior to use in the Great Hall. Expensive table linen and other pieces of tableware were also stored here. Overseeing the Pantry was the 'Pantler'

Buttery comes from the French word for bottle – 'bouteille'. However in medieval times most beverages like ale, mead were stored in barrels – or 'butts' – which were brought up from the cellar and into the buttery to settle before then being transferred into jugs prior to serving at table. Wine was usually stored in a separate cellar.

The man in charge of the Buttery was called a 'butler' and he was responsible for not only the drinks but also the drinking vessels. Both the Pantler and the Butler would answer to the Steward of the house and both rooms would be kept under lock and key.

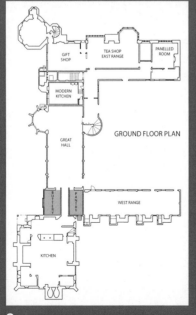

GROUND FLOOR PLAN

GIFT SHOP

TEA SHOP EAST RANGE

PANELLED ROOM

MODERN KITCHEN

GREAT HALL

BUTTERY

PANTRY

WEST RANGE

KITCHEN

Evidence in the form of trefoil-headed moulded bricks on the southern face of the passageway connecting the buttery and pantry to the kitchen suggest that this area may have originally been open, providing a fire-break between the Kitchen and the timber–framed Great Hall beyond. However as the Old Hall evolved this soon became built over forming the room above.

At the servery, food was collected from the two huge hatchways to be taken into the Great Hall. Far from being the job of minions, the servers were high-born young men residing at the hall in order to complete their education-which included instruction in social skills such as horsemanship, fighting arts, music and of course dining etiquette. Similarly, Lord Burgh's sons would have spent time learning these same skills at some other great manor house. This 'exchange programme' was also useful for networking – especially as noble families would be mindful of finding suitable prospective spouses for their own daughters' arranged marriages.

In the west wall of the Servery is a large arch which supports a fireplace in the rooms above.

Interesting Facts

Due to the near famine conditions of the winter of 1816/17, the Old Hall kitchen became a soup kitchen and during the course of sixteen weeks over twenty-thousand meals were passed out to the hungry from the servery hatches. (1816 was the notorious 'year without a summer' when crops failed across huge swathes of the northern hemisphere. This was due to the large amounts of ash accumulated in the atmosphere after the eruption of Mount Tambala in Indonesia.

Rooms above the Servery & Passage

These two rooms have been identified as the 'Stewards Chambers' as in the days of the early Lord Burghs.

The Steward was the Lord of the Manor's most senior, trusted servant who shouldered the myriad day to day responsibilities related to the smooth running of Old Hall estate and beyond. The use of this space for this purpose would make perfect sense as both rooms are within handy reach of the West Range and Kitchen where many of the household servants worked and slept.

The first room, a parlour, is accessed directly by the staircase to the left of the servery hatches. It has a small chimney in the east wall and to the north there is a garderobe/latrine. It is here that the 'muniment' (documents proving ownership of property) and bullion (gold and silver) chests were probably located along with the counting tables. Each morning and afternoon, the Steward and the senior staff held a meeting to discuss business, food and menus as well as general running of the Manor. In the Royal household, and the Lords' private chambers at Parliament, such meetings were held around a table covered in green baize cloth and so known as meetings of the green cloth , and this practice may have been emulated by noble households, like the Burgh's.

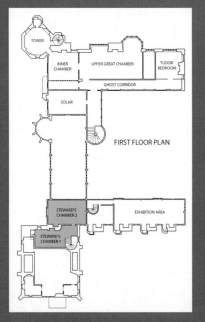

mongst those attending these meetings would be the
teward, Cook and Kitchen Clerk, as well as representatives
om other working departments attached to the Old Hall.
ere clerks would deal with accounting, audit, letters, and
l the other things needed to run His Lordship's business

he adjoining room is accessed from the first and is lit by a
rge window in the north wall. It also has a large fireplace.
his room was almost certainly used by the Steward as his
wn private chamber. Here he likely housed his own office,
omplete with a bed and other luxuries befitting a highly
egarded member of his Lordship's staff. Thomas Burgh II's
teward received the then princely salary of £25 per year.

hese two rooms are probably the same ones listed as being
e first and second 'Brighouse Chambers' in the William
ickman inventory of 1625. The first of these spans the area
etween the Great Hall and the Kitchen above the Servery
st like a bridge or local word 'brig'. This also fits in with
e fact that the Hickman family had owed and used ships
r generations. The term 'bridge' was used on ships for the

command centre and so would equally be of fitting use here
to describe the rooms allotted to their household Steward.

As the Great Hall (and therefore this second room housed
in the cross-wing) was once separated from the kitchen, it
has been suggested that this room might once have served
as the Solar (although how it might have then been
accessed is unclear).

Although the quite grand features of both rooms suggest an
important function, this is somewhat undermined by the
fact that the only apparent access is via the rather mean
stairway more befitting servant status. Coupled with the
close proximity to the lowly status kitchen with its noise and
smell, it is unthinkable that any of Lord Burgh's immediate
family would have chosen to occupy such a place.

This is undoubtedly one of the finest surviving domestic kitchens from the late medieval era. The body of the building, where the fire risk would have been greatest, is built of brick supplemented with timber framing where the risk was minimal. Brick was highly expensive at that time.

Although there is a similarity between the kitchen chimney stacks and those of the west range, with their polygonal brick-built pots, in comparison some of the original kitchen window openings are noticeably lacking in ornamentation - underlining the lowlier function of this building. Also absent from the kitchen is the elaborate moulding of the great hall timberwork, again hinting at its lesser status.

Strategically placed just inside the kitchen entrance is a small two-door room once used by the Clerk to the Kitchen. The Clerk was the man responsible for overseeing supplies of food etc. and managing the numerous kitchen staff and paying their wages. He also kept a watchful eye out for any pilfering. At a time when spices and then sugar were highly expensive, the Clerk also oversaw their careful distribution for use by the cooks, which incidentally at the time was a predominantly male profession.

Kitchen interior

GROUND FLOOR PLAN

On both the north and south walls are two gigantic fireplaces once used for cooking. Both are large enough to have taken an ox for roasting. However in the normal course of events, only the south fireplace would have been used for roasting meat and is equipped with a spit that a young boy would have been employed to turn.

The second fireplace would have been used for cooking such things as boiled meat, vegetables, or 'potage'. Potage was a hearty soup-cum-stew made up basically of what ever odds and ends came to hand in the kitchen, such as off cuts of meat, mixed with vegetables and barley. A warming bowl of pottage would have been very welcoming on a cold day, but one quite literally took 'pot luck' as to what your particular serving would contain.

Although there are purpose-built chimney stacks in the kitchen, up in the roof a louvre similar to that of the Great Hall helped clear the kitchen of excess smoke, steam and fumes and also to let in extra light. The louvre seen today is Victorian.

Built into the west wall is a twin oven, thought to be for pastry, although there has been speculation that there was once a separate bake house in the grounds of the Old Hall. There is not one listed on the 1625 inventory.

Whatever their purpose, all of this type of oven functioned in the same way. To heat the ovens brushwood tied into bundles or 'faggots' was either lit and pushed inside or was placed inside and then ignited by a smaller bundle of burning brushwood called a 'pimp'. The brushwood would have burned extremely quick and hot leaving the bricks inside heated to a high enough temperature for baking. As the brushwood naturally burned out, as much residue as could be quickly raked out was removed – but not too carefully as once the fire had died down the oven would immediately begin to lose precious heat. The uncooked pies or shaped bread dough would quickly be placed on the hot oven floor using a large paddle (often made of light poplar wood) called a 'peel'.

The oven opening would then either be plugged by a thick wooden door shaped to fit (which would have been made ready prior to use by soaking it in a pail of water) or with a

Kitchen exterior

metal plate, either of which could then have been sealed up using some excess bread dough to help keep the heat in. An experienced baker would have known instinctively when the contents were cooked and ready to come out and so then simply chipped away the cooked bread dough seal to open up the door.

Looking up inside the chimney by the ovens, bricks can be seen jutting outwards. These would have been used as foot and handholds for the boys regularly sent up to sweep them.

A corner room at the west end of the north wall (beside the ovens) is currently dressed as a preparation area for baked goods such as bread, with a storage space above for sacks of flour and a pulley system for moving them. In the opposite corner, there is another storeroom dressed as a game larder. Although there must have been such a store somewhere, it is unlikely in reality that it would have been placed here – next to the hot chimney breast. Instead this room may have contained a large copper for boiling water.

The 1625 Inventory mentions a scullery and two larders as being in the Kitchen as well as 'three chambers about the kitchen' which contained beds. Above the Kitchen there is also evidence of further structures, now lost, which may have once provided other places for more servants to sleep

Both the East and West Range are believed to have been built in very quick succession after the Great Hall and Kitchen. Some wood samples seem to suggest that the West Range could be the slightly later building of the two.

Spread over three floors, this area which now has various modern uses was originally intended as a lodging block, complete with numerous garderobes and fire places (which were added after the original timber framed building had been completed). This building would have offered a high standard of comfort for the times.

In the 1625 Inventory, three chambers presumably in this range are assigned to named members of the household of that time – 'Mr. Dalderbig, James Potterton and Mr. Willoughby – (perhaps William Hickman's son and heir also named Willoughby).

During the Victorian era a part of the West Range was used as tenement housing and a pub.

Detail on West Range exterior

Newel Staircase and Landing

The wide spiral staircase and the two storey annex that houses it was probably added at some stage during the Elizabethan era by the Burgh family. (Originally the Solar next to the landing would have to have been accessed by an earlier staircase, perhaps external, directly from the Great Hall's or adjoining Parlour beneath.

Looking through the leaded lights, the raised beds below are a recent reconstruction of a garden from the medieval/Tudor period. They contain a sample of just some of the herbs and plants used at that time for healing and culinary purposes.

During William Hickman's time, there was a wall with a central gate connecting the two ranges and so enclosing the garden into a small courtyard with the Mart Yard beyond. In the Mart Yard – an enclosed outdoor area but in essence an extension of the Old Hall – a three day fair was held each year at Easter and in October.

Hidden from sight beyond the modern day houses to the west is the River Trent. Once the river ran much closer to the Old Hall and Gainsborough was a busy port exporting wool and other goods to Europe. The Lord of the Manor controlled this port and the river – crossing further along (where the bridge is today) from which a large part of the manorial income was generated.

Solar

The Solar, situated in the cross wing above what was once the Great Hall's parlour, can best be described as a rather grand bed-sitting room rather than as an early bedchamber. It would be to this room that the Lord and his Lady, along with perhaps other family members and trusted 'intimate' servants could retire, away from the crowd and noise of the Great Hall.

The meaning of the word 'solar' is often described as being derived from the word 'solaris' – meaning the sun – as most solars are built facing south to make the most of the available natural light but not all are exclusively so. A more likely root for this word is from the French 'seul(e)' which means alone – referring to the privacy such a room might offer.

Most surviving solars from this time had a 'squint' window which allowed the Lord of the Manor to be able to look down upon the Great Hall to observe what those below were doing. As this part of the wall had been adapted in later years for use as a theatre, the original squint window would have been destroyed; therefore a replacement has been inserted in this solar in recent times.

The Solar, dressed with reproduction furniture of the period, provides a taste of what comforts there were to be enjoyed in the late C15th. Wicker fire screens protected noble ladies' delicate pale complexions, as did the reversible bench seat. Chests were used for storage and there is even an oak cupboard containing food and drink. Combined with the warm reed matting and the elaborate wall hangings this lends a rather cosy feeling to the room.

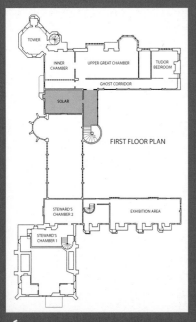

FIRST FLOOR PLAN

Unlike the three-storey West Range, when first built the East Range only had two floors. Instead of suites of rooms, here the larger ceremonial chambers were located. Although this part of the Old Hall was originally timber-framed, the ground floor of the west face was under built in brick during the 19th century. The south gable was encased by brick by William Hickman and according to antiquarian Adam Stark writing in 1813, was once adorned with a sundial dated 1600 and bearing the initials W.H and the inscription 'Deus mi – ut umbra sic vita' – 'My God, life is as a shadow'. Hickman also encased the east exterior with brick and inserted new stone- mullioned windows.

Radical changes were also made to the south end of this range by converting the existing two floors into three and then an additional staircase.

The Lord's private accommodation, which had previously centered upon the tower, was now relocated to the new lighter rooms, at the south end of the building which featured fine fire places. Meanwhile the house's main reception rooms remained located as they had been during the 15th century.

During the 1700's, after the Hickman family had moved to Thonock, the range became the grace and favour apartments of Lord Abingdon.

From 1896 until 1952, the Freemasons used two large rooms on the ground floor of the east range as their Lodge. A Mr. Edmund Dawber resided in the living accommodation at the south end of the range until his death in the 1970's.

Corridor

Houses of this era were usually laid out as a series of linked rooms. The inclusion of a corridor is therefore an unexpected feature for its time.

For more than two centuries at least, reported sightings have been made of a ghostly apparition walking along the corridor towards the north end of the East Range. This female figure all dressed in grey, having reached the leaded lights then turns to disappear through a doorway leading towards the tower. As to whom she might be, many theories abound. Some say that she is a daughter of one of the Lord Burghs, who pined to death after having been forbidden to marry the man she loved. Others believe that she is the ghost of Queen Catherine Howard. If, while visiting the Old Hall you should see her, then please feel free to stop her and ask.

A ghost appears...

Inner Chamber

Once possibly the inner chamber of the Upper Great Chamber, this space now houses the large louvre turret that once sat on the Great Hall roof.

Looking at the outside wall, it is clear to see the original timber-framing now encased in late Tudor/Jacobean brickwork. In fact, with its exposed corridor timbers, this one of the best areas within the Old Hall to gain a clear understanding of how it was constructed and even adapted over time. However, if while visiting you are in any way uncomfortable about being inside a building of such a great age then it is perhaps best not to look up at the ceiling.

Louvre turret

Although it is difficult to determine the exact date that the polygonal tower was added to the East Range, it is quite likely that it was built around the mid 1480's. Maybe Thomas Burgh II having been elected as a Knight of the Garter under Richard III or perhaps his summons to the House of Lords in 1487 (after being created First Baron Gainsborough by Henry VII) would both have been occasions worthy of marking by such a fine addition to the family seat.

Although very military-looking in architecture, features such as the large widows on the top floor and the easy access to the lower rooms suggest that this tower's use was always intended as domestic rather than defensive.

The internal layout of the tower comprises three separate floors containing a single room with a fireplace and an adjoining garderobe, which are accessed by a spiral staircase of forty-five stone steps.

During the Burgh family's ownership, these rooms are thought to have formed a part of the lord's family apartments.

In the distant past it was possible to see much further from the top of the tower than today However, perhaps not as far as Adam Stark claims in his 'History of Gainsborough' written in 1813:

'The top of the tower commands a very extensive prospect of the whole of the course of the Trent, nearly to where it joins the Humber, the hills at Aukborough and Burton-Stather being easily seen; and from it the approach of any vessel is perfectly to be distinguished.'

The tower would have been very useful when looking out for ships on their way to Gainsborough – especially if they were gun-ships armed with cannon as during the English Civil War! Today there is a pleasant panorama of Gainsborough town, the parish church of All Saints and beyond.

Interesting fact:

There are documentary hints that there may have once been two towers at Gainsborough Old Hall. After preaching in the grounds of the hall in June1786, John Wesley wrote: 'One of the towers is said to have been built in the reign of King Stephen, above six hundred years ago...'

Intriguingly William Burgh's will of 1496 also talks of a 'lowe towre': *"And also I will if my sonn Thomas life at the day of my buriell that he have... the bedde of the lowe towre and hanging and counterpoint of the said towre..."*

Why should Burgh have qualified his description with this adjective 'lowe' if there was only the one tower?

If there was indeed a second tower it does not appear on the 1625 Hickman inventory as being occupied – although the remains of a disused tower could have quite possibly been converted into a 'horse-mill' – of which there is one mentioned as being within the Old Hall grounds.

Adam Stark in his 'History of Gainsborough' does not mention a second tower. Instead he apparently ignores that possibility by quoting, quite scathingly, from a poem from The Lady's Museum, of October 1799:

> 'Mark where yon mould'ring edifice appears,
> The shatter'd remnant of devouring years;
> E'en now the towers a grandeur still display
> Which time itself can never take away.'

Where this 'missing' tower, if it existed, could have stood is a mystery, and likely to remain so as much of the Old Hall's once extensive grounds have since been built upon.

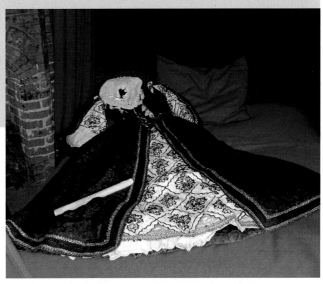

Upper Great Chamber

Throughout the C15th, C16th and on into the C17th, the Upper Great Chamber would have been used as the main ceremonial room on this floor by both the Burghs and the Hickmans. After the departure of the Hickman family to Thonock this room was still accorded high status.

During the C19th the wooden frame of the ceiling of the Upper Great Chamber was raised by about 75cm and the exterior brickwork built up accordingly. At that time the room was not divided as it is today and was used as the town's public assembly room.

The gothic-style fireplace, decorated with the Burgh family emblem- the 'Maynfer- or mailed fist and roses (suggesting the 'War of the Roses') was also added at this time. Two carved wooden panels above the doorways are of the same date.

Today one of the most notable things about this impressive space is the numerous portraits of past members of the Hickman and Bacon families.

Fireplace detail

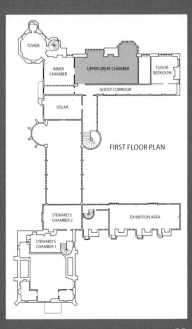

FIRST FLOOR PLAN

Created by William Hickman, this room could possibly be the one described as being his bed chamber in the 1625 inventory. The room today is dressed very much as it would have been in Sir William's lifetime.

The bed (although not the original) is very fitting owing to its intricate carvings depicting such biblical scenes as 'Cain killing Abel' and 'Adam and Eve in the Garden of Eden' as well as several beautiful angels. The head of the bed also has a secret compartment hidden amongst the carvings.

Above the bedroom (and now used as staff offices) is a suite of smaller rooms- almost certainly the 'nursery', and 'high chamber' also mentioned next in the inventory. The fact that there is a nursery may help to date closely these particular adaptations. Sir William's first wife Agnes had been childless during her previous marriage. Widowed and older, Agnes had remained childless during her second marriage and up until her death in February of 1600. William remarried almost immediately and soon needed a nursery to house his growing brood of young children

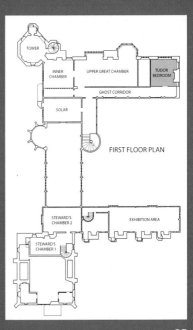

FIRST FLOOR PLAN

Panelled Room & Tyrwhitt Room

This room could possibly be the 'litle dineing parlor' of the 1625 inventory as the next item is described as 'the litle side parlor'. The creation of this room and the small one adjoing it are the result of the reordering of this end of the East Range during William Hickman's renovations. This is the only room to have retained its fine oak panelling.

According to Thomas Burgh II's will of 1496, this part of the range then contained a parlour, an inner parlour with an adjoining chamber. However 'reconstructing' the original layout of this ground floor area is difficult owing to the many changes it has undergone. Added to this, Hickmans rearrangement has also since been changed. Therefore, the original layout of much of the ground floor is uncertain.

In the small side chamber – now known as the Tyrwhitt Room – there is an intriguing piece of Tudor graffiti, thought to have been written during the 1541 visit by one of Henry VIII's courtiers. In the Hickmans' time this chamber may have served as a 'closet' where a close stool might have been kept – which is understandable considering the apparent lack of garderobes in this part of the building.

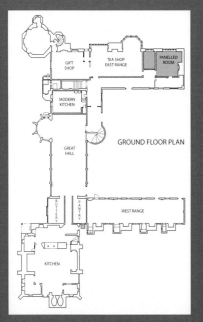

GROUND FLOOR PLAN

Gift and Tea Shop Area

At least a part of this ground floor area now serving as the Gift Shop (where the wall painting is) was listed as being the 'Garden Parlour' on the 1625 inventory. This would tie in nicely with both its position adjacent to the original Old Hall gardens and the apparent subject matter of the painting extending across both the plaster and beams of one wall. Stylistically this mural dates from the early 17th century. There is an earlier but much more extensive wall painting, similar in style and execution, at Ellys House, Great Ponton, near Grantham in Lincolnshire, which gives an idea of how exquisite the one at Gainsborough might once have been.

Gardens and exterior

No visit to Gainsborough Old Hall would be complete without stopping to stroll around the grounds and to take in the wonderful architectural features of the building's fascinating exterior.

On the east face wall of the East Range brickwork are four curious alcoves that never fail to intrigue visitors. These recesses are called 'bee boles' and each is just big enough to hold a hive made of coiled-straw or 'skep' as they are called. Beekeepers in England used these skeps before the introduction of modern-style wooden bee hives in the C19th.

Devoted volunteers of the Friends of Gainsborough Old Hall's gardening group lovingly tend the flowerbeds and parterre.

Wall painting at Ellys House, Great Ponton, near Grantham in Lincolnshire

Bee bole containing a skep

The Old Hall – a true survivor

Throughout her long existence, Gainsborough Old Hall has intermittently suffered from neglect, decay and near extinction. Yet through thoughtful and timely intervention, each occasion she has survived to come though such adversity stronger than before.

One such period of neglect, which had begun in the second half of the 1700s, led Thomas Miller to reminisce:

"It had been let off for a long time in separate rooms for shops and dwelling- places, to the great disgrace of the owner, for it was once one of the finest old baronial mansions that could be found within many miles... You peeped in and saw its great ground floor apartments occupied by joiners, and coopers, and bricklayers – depositories for their lime, hair and bricks – and you turned away in disgust.

In one of the few stained-glass windows that remained over the low broad archway, which commanded a view of the garden behind, and no doubt had, in former times, been beauty's bower, a mass of unsightly rags were stuffed through the centre of the deep-dyed shield."

On that occasion, it was Henry Bacon Hickman who came to the rescue and between 1847 and 1849 had engaged Ibbetson to carry out repairs and the restoration of the Great Hall.

Again, in 1878 repairs and renovations were undertaken, this time by the new owner, Henry's great-nephew, Hickman Beckett Bacon.

By the end of WWII, the Old Hall had fallen yet again into a state of dilapidation with the Great Hall, West Range and the north end of the East Range in serious danger of collapse.

It was at this time that a dedicated, forward-thinking group of local people, under the leadership of Harold Witty Brace, formed themselves into a voluntary organisation to carry out urgent repairs themselves to save the building. Thus 'The Friends of the Old Hall Association' came onto being with the noble aim of saving, preserving and promoting Gainsborough Old Hall so that it might carry on being enjoyed and appreciated by many future generations. The association is as active today as ever it was in its pursuits and always welcoming of new members.

Today, Lincolnshire County Council manages Gainsborough Old Hall while English Heritage owns it and cares for the fabric of the building. Much of the hall's furniture and paintings still belong to the Bacon family.

Events

At Gainsborough Old Hall history matters and so throughout the year colourful and exciting events are regularly held.

From Medieval re-enactors and crafts people 'inhabiting' the Old Hall, bringing alive a past way of life and filling the air with the cooking aromas of long-forgotten dishes to vintage car rallies, there is always something going on for all the family to enjoy. Added to this, are often a variety of talks and presentations hosted at the Old Hall throughout the year.

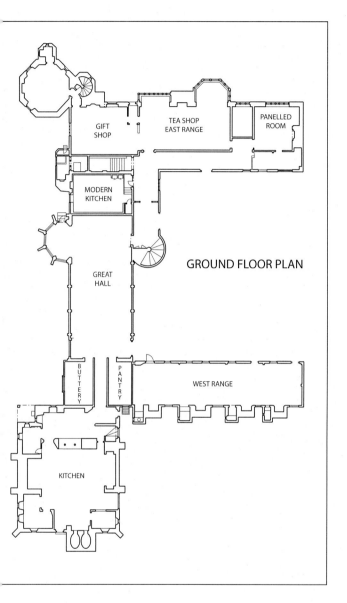

GROUND FLOOR PLAN

GIFT SHOP

TEA SHOP EAST RANGE

PANELLED ROOM

MODERN KITCHEN

GREAT HALL

BUTTERY

PANTRY

WEST RANGE

KITCHEN

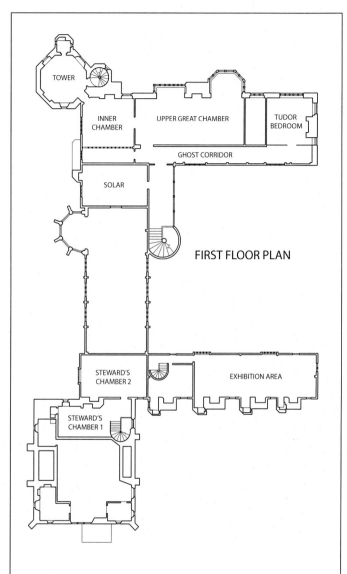

FIRST FLOOR PLAN

TOWER

INNER CHAMBER

UPPER GREAT CHAMBER

TUDOR BEDROOM

GHOST CORRIDOR

SOLAR

STEWARD'S CHAMBER 2

EXHIBITION AREA

STEWARD'S CHAMBER 1

Glossary

Corbel – a piece of stone, wood, or metal, often in the form of a bracket, projecting from the side of a wall and serving to support a cornice, the spring of an arch, etc.

Close stool – a commode or type of portable toilet.

Garderobe – is a medieval toilet emptying into a pit below. Soon it was discovered that fumes emanating up from the pit could be harnessed to kill off the lice and fleas that commonly inhabited ones clothing at this time. Garments, therefore, were routinely hung up in this toilet area for treatment thus giving it its name. The pits were regularly dug out and emptied by hand and the hapless people given that task were called gong farmers. Alternative names for the Garderobe were the privy, jakes, draught, and gong.

Tracery – ornamental work of interlacing or branching lines of stonework used to break up a larger space within a window or 'light'. As seen in the Great Hall bay window – each larger arched 'light' has been split into two parts.

Trefoil-headed – ornamental decoration or figure resembling a threefold leaf

Vault – an arched roof, ceiling, or covering of masonry.

Acknowledgements

Gainsborough Old Hall

Lincolnshire County Council

Lincoln Archives

FOHA

Roger Vorhauer

Brita Lakeman

Brita Lakeman

Lord Burgh Retinue

Dr Philip Lindley

Rich Hines

Designed and produced by Domtom Publishing Ltd

Text by Sue Allen

Printed in Great Britain by DPS Partnership Ltd

www.dpsltd.net

ALSO BY SUE ALLEN:

The Mayflower Maid

The first part of the New World Trilogy

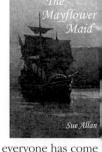

400 years ago a group of like minded men and women fled England and religious persecution to start a new life on a new continent – America.

One woman's story begins here....

In the infant colony of Plymouth in 1623 a woman lies consumed with fever. In her delirium she insists her name is not the one everyone has come to know and love her by.

The story of Dorothy's tragic journey amongst the Pilgrim Fathers is a vivid and moving account of a pivotal moment in history. The story of how she became the Mayflower Maid is an unforgettable tale of love and loss set amidst the strife and religious bigotry of Seventeenth Century England.

Tudor Rose

The story of the reformation, told through the voice of a woman of the times

Lady Rose Hickman was an extraordinary woman of courage, who lived through one of the most turbulent periods in English History and survived the reigns of two Tudor Kings and nine Tudor queens to tell her remarkable tale...

From her father's Bible smuggling days at the Catholic Court of King Henry VIII, her brothers courageous voyages of exploration, to her final years at Gainsborough Old Hall...

Under Queen Elizabeth, Lady Rose and her family suffered persecution as Puritan reformers and gave sanctuary to the Separatists who spawned the Mayflower Pilgrims of America.

Steps along the Mayflower Trail

Steps along the Mayflower Trail is not intended to be a book about the Mayflower Pilgrims – or Separatists, as they were known before their voyage to America.

Instead, this book has been written as a reference companion for those who are already familiar with the Separatists' saga – but who are perhaps not so familiar with the places that feature in it.

'Steps along the Mayflower Trail', sets out to illuminate those villages, towns and buildings in the three counties of Lincolnshire, Yorkshire and Nottinghamshire, that played major roles in their odyssey. These are places that many of the Separatists would have once known as home.